T5-CCJ-523

QUESTIONING THE COMET

Questioning the Comet

Stevie Krayer

gomer

First Impression – 2004

ISBN 1 84323 346 0

© Stevie Krayer

Stevie Krayer has asserted her right under the Copyright, Design and Patents Act, 1988, to be identified as Author of this Work.

All rights reserved. No part of this book may be reproduced, stored in a retrieval system, or transmitted in any form or by any means, electronic, electrostatic, magnetic tape, mechanical, photocopying, recording or otherwise without permission in writing from the publishers, Gomer Press, Llandysul, Ceredigion.

This book is published with the financial support of the Welsh Books Council.

Printed in Wales at
Gomer Press, Llandysul, Ceredigion SA44 4QL

To Rene and Gus Krayer
with thanks for over half a century of plutzing

ACKNOWLEDGEMENTS

Some of these poems have appeared or been accepted for publication in the following magazines: *The Friend*, *Friends Quarterly*, *New Welsh Review*, *Orbis*, *Planet*, *Poetry Salzburg Review*, *Quaker Monthly*, *Rialto* and *Stand*.

I am grateful to Glenys Cour for the cover image and design, and to Wally Jenkins for his work on the cover.

CONTENTS

Learning the Language

Aeron Poems

1. Searching for the Source

We hunt first on the map
smoothing out the wrinkles
till the copperplate lines
of hedge and contour run clear.

Etched on hillsides
the flèched imprint
of predatory conifers
and their metal kin.

To the east, Teifi
scores boldly through a lake
of submerged blue alligators.
But upstream Aeron

dissipates into tentative
doodlings. Which one
is the authentic signature?
She seems possessed

by quantum elusiveness,
evading observation in
a Brownian swirl of contours.
Maybe we need a bigger map.

Things on the ground
are no clearer. At Blaenpennal bridge
we jump from the car, stare down
at the sepia water, which is unlabelled.

A lane takes us up and up
into the wind.
                    Almost
we forget our quest,

distracted by zinc barn-doors
that fidget uneasily, the peevishness
of a rotting garden gate,
the keening of phone wires.

Oaks roar, as if on the sky's muddy pitch
the gale were scoring try after try;
the terraces in their expansiveness
throw handfuls of torn leaves into the drizzle

2. The Source

In twenty miles we pass
from woods and gardens
to a raw upland of yellow bogs
and conifer plantations.

The hilltop is busy:
sheepdog trials, a radio mast,
cows, bungalows. But there
is the lake,

small and unruffled
in a sanctuary of marshes;
we cannot reach the point
where Aeron is born.

At the top end, the energetic spring
that feeds Llyn Eiddwen is nameless
and necessary as the sperm
that penetrates the egg.

But it's false to speak of birth.
Aeron is no more a baby here
than at her gracious mouth.
The whole of her length and age

coexists at once, forever renewed
as it was long before the ruins
on the shoreline of the lake
were new-built pens and hopes.

This narrow, deep twist
of peat-ale in a throat of grasses
is the first verse of a torah scroll
you may begin anywhere.

3. The Name

She swells, dwindles, clots, clouds with colour.
Yet we who live by the river keep forgetting
the strangeness, return a routine greeting
day by day to the familiar mutter.
We know her name; she's just another neighbour.

What fools us is the way we find her supine
each morning in the same bed – but that's
water's indolence. When a river surfeits
it will move on, wiping clean the canon
like hopscotch lines forgotten in the rain.

Those who once dared baptise a babe so old
did not mistake naming for taming. They called her
after the Goddess at the ford,
insatiable for men in sex and war;
the Washer and the water held in awe.

What power is in names, *frodorion*,*
that they take root among your own
deep roots, ivy you to your ground,
so you must always chant them
wherever you meet, twine them in every poem?

* *brodorion*: Native inhabitants of a *bro* or neighbourhood – see also p. 21.

4. Floods

Each night they're on TV, hair slicked with wet,
describing drily for the interviewer
the sofa that's a bed for cress, the carpet
mulched with mud, the larder now a sewer.
Sooner or later the dyke of calm gives way;
tears fill the throat and wash the words away.

It's no Limpopo, but when Aeron balloons
there's the same warning in that wall-eyed stare
from fields transformed to sloblands and lagoons:
some forces can't be fenced, no-one's secure;
though rainbows follow, they will later fade;
even the comfortable reap what they sowed.

The stain of flood or blood gets scrubbed away;
the tattoo on the soul is there to stay.

5. Plas Gelli*

[For RT]

There are no ghosts at Gelli;
only a peaceful past
shading the permeable present.

Trees long felled add their silence
to the deep-chested vespers
of the remaining beeches.

Monks have left behind
the prayer of their domesticity
and a garden wall.

An arched casement still looks out
from high in the sycamore trunk, though
a tawny owl no longer sits in it.

No bench now under the looped boughs
where a poet lapped still-warm milk
holding the tumbler in both hands.

Kitchen, cowshed, neat rows of tools.
What change in human need
can make a barrier of three hundred years?

No grief so haunting
but could find rest here, waking
to the daylight fact of happiness.

---

* Home to Dylan and Caitlin Thomas between 1941-43 and the place where
their daughter Aeronwy was probably conceived.

6. The People

Save me, O God,
for the waters have come up to my neck.
I sink in deep mire,
where there is no foothold.

Psalm 69

Ignore the mansions: this was a place
where a man of substance was one
who left a chest of linen, a dozen sheep,
two nags and a couple of crockpots. Most
lived low to the ground: under tree-roots
and thatch, squeezed between mud walls.
From as soon as they could see
until it was too dark to see any longer
they worked the soil. Spare moments
and small children were a chance to earn
a few extra pence by knitting stockings.
Easy to think such brutal toil made clods
of the poor, as it blunted the forks and spades
that were their only heirlooms.

But they lifted each other, pooling resourcefulness:
four might share a net and bring back herring.
Cargoes came to the small landing-place
of Aberaeron – salt, corn, coal
and books. Somehow these human oxen
found three months for learning
in winter, when the Circulating School
came to their village. Decades before the first book
was published on Welsh soil,
the vicar of Cilcennin had to beg
for hundreds of bibles to meet
the insatiable demand. Was it for piety
or to read of a young shepherd-bard
whom God made King of Israel?

7. Meeting with the Mesolithic

Take this flint in your hand: a mountain ridge
no bigger than a skimming stone,
satin beneath your thumb, a little warm,
as if you touched the moment of its knapping:

the ice-shield not long melted,
Wales' crushed ribs freed for a first
intake of breath that goes on for millenia.
Trees, grasses, creatures creeping back.

Then come humans. Aeron, filling itself
from Eiddwen's inkwell, writes a new story
under the Mynydd Bach – their holy writ.
They gather its riches, guide their lives by it.

But they are not the last. Their unfenced home
tells of trust that will some day prove fatal.
The valley has become a palimpsest –
our time's exhaust may dull it to a scrawl.

8. The Poets

Iago Trychrug

Born where the railway would run through Ciliau
a hundred years later; when he was two
his mother died. Steel riddled him long before
he was apprenticed to the blacksmith.

The master's rod of iron drove him early
to London. Better the gunmetal Thames
drilled through grey dockyards, than the mocking
bloom on Aeron's breasts.

The soot-blackened hammer of his pain
forged the poet and the minister.
His best-wrought poem scourged
the skinflints who cut his chapel stipend.

Did he ever dream of the valley, kapok-lined
with mist, feathered with woods, the nest of wrens?

Dinah Davies

Up in the valley's heaven, birds perform
their sacraments – buzzards and kites
outspread in deadly cruciform;
the short, beseeching flights
of chaffinches, swifts shot direct
from the Spirit's crossbow.
But Dinah Davies had too much self-respect
to let her fancy pierce the frosted window.

And if Nantcwnlle Chapel ceiling were
not nearly enough sky for such as her
she paid no heed, but kept her inner gaze
fixed hawklike on the pulpit all her days;
eyes closed, with sharp yet merciful observation,
saw through the all-too-human congregation.

*Beirdd y Mynydd Bach**

I stand at their monument and look down
over lake, ruins, farms, hills. I see beauty
but they saw neighbours. All the landscape
was named, known, intimate as the hand
in which they versified their *bro*.
Each hedge-thorn and fencepost recognised
and greeted them, every day the same
since before memory. All spoke
the same ancient tongue, born of tussling
together with the stubborn scrubland.

My foreign words skate lovingly across fields
smoothing away the detail as they pass.
I start acclimatising, taking root here.
Like a rhododendron in Snowdonia.

* Poets of the Little Mountain.

Iaith Fyw
(Living Language)

Up in the deep litter
inside my head
newborn language
is being catlicked
into life.

Words hum and enter
waveringly, dance
to each other.
Honey drips from the beams;
I catch it on my tongue.

Even at night,
umbrella-winged
phrases flit about
or hang upside-down
from my clothes.

Memoirs of Ruth Mynachlog

Before the metalled road that brought us here,
before fences or ditches, or the noise
of tractors and turbines, was the wild land:
y rhos, y gors, y waun.

How to see past the concrete now
to the rough uplands of the pathless past,
scrubby with hardship? Even the tell-tale tracks
of what was once so commonplace –

Red knuckles, calluses, feet gnarled by clogs –
have dissolved with the limbs they scarred.
Give thanks, then, for those few who took the trouble
to mark the way with cairns of patient words.

Ynys Lochtyn

Cowled with rain that hung in long grey pleats,
the storm-systems were lined up for twenty miles
across an amphitheatre of bulging water.
To the chant of gales, the gasps of flagellant surf,
they overstepped the rocks and swept inland
to browbeat and dishearten all they caught
unsheltered – poppies, hens or human souls.

Only the dolphins, wavelike, went on cresting
undismayed; and the heart leapt with them.
The glossy biceps of the sea, they flexed:
black rainbows, playful covenants of hope.

The Secret Room

[For BPW]

It stands as it stood
raised up to God
on the heights where its walls were quarried.

Glimpsed through the panes,
planks and paint-cans –
ominous signs.

A straggle of modern Quakers
mills at the doorstep
ignored by a thousand acres.

Look what he gave up
for his faith! exclaims one.
What would I have done?

Across slopes coppered with bracken
the wind echoes the question.
Then it's back to the minibus.

This poem refers to Bryn Mawr, on the slopes of Cadair Idris, the home of
one of the first Quakers in Wales, Rowland Ellis.

Because of our Coming

I never hear the dawn chorus. It's the windows
coming home that bid me from sleep. At once
I am skin-full of the knowledge before words –
who I am and where I am, and who
is purring heavily at my back, unconscious.
Each morning I sip tea and read myself awake,
dress in the same frayed shirt and jeans,
baptise my boots in a dew-field that tips eastward
so the sun spills in across a wooded brim.

Later, we walk the cliffs. Where a collapsed
lip of earthwork rings a sweep of turf
with ancient presence, we sit with sandwiches
and watch blue pulses plough the milky sea.
Dinghies and fishing boats clamber the swells,
all sailing away from us, small engine noises
bleached clean as driftwood, slowly fading.
I half expect a boat against the flow, coming
for me straight out of the western horizon,
painted blue, perhaps, with a square sail
and a figurehead. I'll know it when it comes.

Instead we go home. It's time to harvest
crab-apples. Squalls of flushed pebbles
are shaken down – we race the hens
for them, bucket them indoors,
cut them to shards, pulp them, hang
the broken mass on a nail to well and drip:
the season saved, transmuted to rosy liquor.

At last we sit down together for the meal
we have been moving towards all day.
We light the candles of each other's talk.
My delight is to bring trove from the garden,
elaborate it for the table; his to eat
with appetite big as his heart.
I am the dinner of herbs he has preferred.

Searching the Archives

Welsh Hills – Jerusalem Hills

September. The late flush of midges
in the sunny air tempts the swallows
to stay a little longer, though they keep up
a constant clicking of alerts along the wires.

The green clouds overhanging the cliff
sharpen at close range into barbs, endangering
bare arms and legs – gorse, blackthorn, hawthorn
(wind-pruned to an outstretched *sieg heil*
forbidding the way), nettles, coils of bramble.
Even the bracken scrapes past, harshly indifferent.

Heat carries thought eastwards to other hills
that bristle with more pointed threats. In this bracken
a Maquis could hide, at cost of laceration;
but how dissolve into that naked clay
where every trail betrays itself from far away
and there's little choice but to resist in the open.

Two scraps of debatable land. I can claim neither.
Yet both hillscapes have seeded themselves
in my eye, clawed roots deep into me
so my heart shuttles, imprinted like a migrant bird.

Children of the Revolution

Just as the Celtic monks with their devotions
made thin places for the spirit, so you,
my parents and your comrades, worried
at the barriers in dusty assembly rooms
with your tombola, your threadbare jumble,
your weak tea in thick white china, marging
and jamming loaves, slicing Dundee,
raising pennies for a thin daily.

You gave your faith, your time, your energy
in a daily litany of lit. and argument:
matins of the Sunday soapbox, lauds
of the doorstep. Branch meetings
were your vespers, censed with Woodbines.
Your festivals were demos, when your hearts
were lifted by the thousands who joined
the celebration, dancing in the city square.

You looked East and saw a star –
emblem of working people, not divinities.
You believed there was a place on earth
where *all* the carpenters' sons were exalted
for the astral pull of birth had been eclipsed.
And so it could happen all over the world.
Heaven on earth proved a chimera; and yet
somewhere there's still a star that guides you.

Menorah

1. Pesach: the Promised Land

Sitting down for the Seder, we fill the room
like broken biscuits, a tribe for this one evening
round matzos piled on a starch-white tablecloth.

And is this the promised land? this narrow,
sunless, bickering semi-basement
rented from Uncle Solly, who has prospered;

this dank passage, lean-to outhouse,
cramped scullery where Nana performs
exquisite kitchen observances:

verenikes, chopped liver, melting strudel.
Tonight, halved eggs are eyes sunk in tears.
The kneidlach float, adrift on golden soup.

Meanwhile she holds inside her
stoically, like a prolapsed womb,
the ocean that separates her from her sisters.

The grandfathers grieve too. Moishe looks back –
the territory he left is now his Canaan,
Lenin his Moses, Uncle Joe his Joshua.

Mendel dreams at the sweatshop bench
of a kibbutz in Eretz Israel, but never dreams
that Jews on their own soil will forget how to share.

So, not quite the promised land, but a foothold
on Mount Nebo, from where the grandmothers
look out over a land flowing with diplomas.

Here there are council flats, here policemen
carry no guns, here goyim have stood with Jews
to stem a flood of blackshirts.

They live to see us little ones go beyond them
in stethoscope or wig, suckled on freedom,
fed with the thin honey of acceptance.

Behind lies something worse than Pharaoh's slavery.
Masha and Esther-Soorah have settled for England:
better a safe place now than a fabled Jerusalem.

2. Shavuot: Waiting for Pentecost

This is the hungry season; clothes hang on us
like the shrivelled skin on the last few
apples in the loft. This is the season
when milk dries up – fifty days can measure
a baby's life. Edgily, we watch the wheat
fill out. We watch the sky. We wait.

Hunger is a wilderness plagued by mirage.
There are no reliable tracks. Like our forebears
after Egypt, quarrelling in the desert
that freedom turned out to be, we cannot yet
see to the end of this. It takes a full belly
to give thanks for the skim milk of the Law.

Hard to have faith. Are we awaiting
something to come or something
gone for good? Like the followers
of that rabbi who was crucified
we wait even while reason says
the dead cannot rise again.

The round of festivals makes us a promise
that fullness will return when it is due,
that rainbow's ends meet underground.
The first fruits are bound to reappear,
and the fire to rekindle. But God
is capricious. How can we be sure?

3. Sukkot: the Sukka

I am the Sukka: ramshackle and leafy,
no deep foundations. Come to me
for feasting and laughter
but not for security. I endanger
no-one, but I can't keep out the rain.
My roof and walls are cut boughs.
I let in the light; I am trusting
and full of gaps. You can roost in me
if you weigh no more than small birds.
The love brims up in me and leaks out
between my ribs and trickles down to earth.
If I were not so temporary
this would in time cut deep grooves in my sides.
It dissipates in the soil, and I never know
what has happened to it. When the time comes
to dismantle me, all that will be left
is an oblong of trampled ground, and soon
the grass and nettles will green over that.
I am like the wedding canopy; I can only
stretch forth a blessing. After that
it's up to those I shaded for a while.

4. Rosh Hashanah: Turning

As far south as Israel, now is the time of year
when leaves are turning. Olives and grain
are siloed, and our hemisphere
begins its elliptic voyage from the sun.
The Jews have set aside these darker days
for *teshuvah* – the bending of our gaze
inward and rearward. To move ahead
the only way is back. We must confront
the mess we left on land, the wrong we did.
To be forgiven, we must first repent.

Below deck, something shifts its viscid weight,
burdens the sea, drags us out of true.
We tanker-navigators of the North
prefer to forge straight lines, forget
that we must follow the curve of earth.
Unwilling to change course, we argue
such manoeuvres are too costly, and too late.
Soon we will admit we are askew.
Soon we will stand and watch as our disgrace
pumps by the tonne across the water's face.

It may be so, it may already be too late
to go about – beneath our keel the lane
is narrowing like the light. And yet
the earth renews its circle round the sun,
and Rosh Hashanah comes unfailingly
as days begin to dwindle. A New Year:
another chance to choose a better way,
repair the ravaged land, reclaim old error,
change breaks to bridges on that holy Day
of Atonement when neighbour joins with neighbour.

5. Chanukkah: Lighting the Menorah

One for the miracle of the Temple lamp;
One for the match that kindles the sabbath;
One for the phoenix that rose from the firestorm
    – scorched, stunted, crazy, but alive;
One for the midwives from other tribes
    who slipped behind the lines of night to deliver us;
One for the candles that press back the dark
    of every faith's winter;
One for the chutzpah of Prometheus;
One for every human soul, akin and alone.
Seven wise eyes that see past and future,
Seven gold almonds that honey the air,
Shine of seven unshed tears.
They'll hoop the room
    in light that leaps
        as long as wax may last.

6. Purim: Casting Lots

This happened in the days of Ahasuerus.
Since Mordecai the Jew would not bow down
Haman decreed the Jews should all be massacred.
Esther had the chance to save her people
by risking not just crown and privilege
but life itself, if she displeased the king.
Esther demurred. These were the words that swayed her:
Who knows? perhaps you came to royal dignity
for just such a time as this. Then Esther said:
'I will go to the king. And if I die, I die.'

This happened in Poland, 1942.
The SS gave the order to assemble
in the ghetto square; Reuben, already safe
in the shelter prepared by his Christian friend,
went back to share his family's fate.
And this happened in the line for the 'hot baths':
when the moment came, one girl panicked.
A certain Mother Maria took her place.
And long ago, there was a man who let himself
be crucified, to show love has no limits.

These are less heroic times, no doubt.
Yet isn't life saying to us at every moment
Who knows, perhaps it was for this
you came to the throne of your humanity?
Look at the acres of canvas each of us
is given to paint the portrait of ourselves –
look at the palette and the wealth of tools.
Only the time is short. Yet a moment
is all it takes to choose life, whether it be
a fly, a people or your integrity.

7. Shabbat: the Seventh Day

The ones who created Jahweh made the sabbath —
a reward of rest for work well done.
And after Eden that's how the deal
was understood — no sweat, no sabbath.
Ever since then, we've found a million ways
to celebrate Shabbat, from the bride
who rides with sunset as it sweeps
round the world, to the moment
when the shovel is rested against the wall,
the cigarette lit and the cleared ditch contemplated.

But some have seen a seventh day
when the counting falls silent. A man
will look up from his furious trance
of butchery and realise how weary he is.
He'll put down the cleaver, wipe his bloody hands
on his apron, and go home.
Upstairs, he'll take off his filthy workclothes
and throw them in a corner.
Then, showered and dressed
in a fresh shirt, he'll go down to the family.

The best damask cloth will be laid
with silver cutlery and a glossy chollah,
the candles not yet lit. For the Sabbath guest
is still awaited — the enemy
who stands at the door and knocks.
A wishful thought, you say.
But haven't you heard
about Oswaldtwistle,
and the German POWs
who came to Christmas dinner?

Pesach: Passover, a seven-day festival celebrating the liberation of Israel from Egyptian slavery. Takes place at about the same time as Easter. The Seder is the festival ritual on the first night, which includes the special food eaten, e.g. 'matzo' (a large, square water-biscuit), commemorating the unleavened bread which the Israelites took into the desert.

Shavuot: festival of 'first fruits', also celebrates the giving of the Law to Moses on Sinai. Otherwise known as Pentecost (Greek for 50) because it falls 50 days (seven weeks) after Pesach.

Sukkot: harvest festival. Traditionally Jews build a 'sukka' or makeshift hut and eat their meals in it during the festival, to commemorate the wandering in the wilderness after the flight from Egypt.

Rosh Hashanah: the Jewish New Year, which falls in October. Part of the period known as the Days of Awe, leading up to Yom Kippur (Day of Atonement), a solemn period of self-purification when Jews seek to be reconciled to God and to all those whom they may have injured or offended during the year.

Chanukkah: a midwinter festival of lights commemorating the purification of the Temple in 164 BCE after its desecration by Antiochus Epiphanes IV. The Menorah, or seven-branched (sometimes nine-branched) candlestick, is particularly associated with this festival. An additional candle is lit each day of the festival.

Purim: festival based on the biblical story of Esther saving the Jews from a genocide plot in the reign of Ahasuerus.

Shabbat: Sabbath. The Jewish sabbath runs from sunset on Friday to sunset on Saturday. It is customary to have a special plaited loaf on Shabbat, made with white flour and eggs: the 'chollah'.

Romanian Grandmothers

[For Feli and Florin]

This one is silver, slight, a smile that curves
like a waning moon in a headscarf.
Back bowed within the bindings of her apron,
her knotted fingers gently play
grace notes on the strings of the loom.

The other's face is a round sun beaming
smiles full of gold; she's plump and sweet
as butter. She makes things grow,
has patience for the slow unfolding
of dahlias, quilling, needlepoint.

In the cobbled courtyard, among the piglets
and hens, a mobile phone is bleating.
The little girls drift off, indifferent
to the craftwork that already looks
like relics in the living hands that made it.

This is the land my own grandmother left
eighty years ago. She took her thimble
but the skill died with the supple fingers.
She too knew how to make those radiant smiles
that light the world when tapestries have faded.

First Steps in Stepmothering

At some point of strayed attention
I lost the path and found myself alone.
The Sugar Loaf slowly
straightened itself up
to meet my face. Fingers clinging
to clumps of grass, toes wedged
on an inch of ledge, I hung there
with several decades' leisure to observe
the lifeless colour of the soil and grass,
the way the mountainside was wrinkled
with sheeptracks, all crossing
left to right, none going up.

It seemed I could not ever bear to leave
my crabhold; but some neuronal flicker
told me I was no longer paralysed.
Retreat was out – the only way
was onwards. As I achieved the top,
gasping, the three of them
were waiting like an ambush. But when
I burst into tears, little Dan
put out his arms, soothed me like a father.

Poem for my Stepdaughter's Birthday

You were already waiting for me
in the café, so that I saw your picture
for a moment behind plate-glass:
sheathed in your soft business armour
hair gathered in the Roman fashion, high
on the crown to leave unmasked
your coined profile in all its queenly candour.

Behind the aegis of sophistication
I see a child on a hilltop, stoically
battling for breath, cutting short her tears
whatever the cause – cut knee or split family.
You've always plunged without hesitation
into your pleasures – but there's
a spearpoint for those who think you easy prey.

Without hauteur, Minerva of Finsbury Park,
you hug me to your warmth, too gracious
to remind me I'm a supplicant. As you talk
of conferences, appraisals, presentations,
I see the owl half-hidden on your shoulder,
the wild creature who has always been there
watching the world, weaving its life in the dark.

Wedding

[for Siân and Pete]

Stardate 200701

Today, after a tricky approach
we touched down safely on Planet Wedding.
Most have landed by now, in this alien place
where the plumage is so brilliant
and the food all unaccustomed delicacies.
We stroll, marvelling, through panelled halls,
deerparks, gardens. Fountains dance, blossom
confettis the lawns. We are welcomed
as honoured guests, to be cherished
as though we were the first who ever landed.

Stardate 210701

Representatives of the two colonies
are assembled and expectant. Theirs are strangers;
our own people too have turned suddenly strange
in this moment of caught breath. Their man, our woman
are transfiguring before our eyes
under the planet's influence. How long have they
been growing to this poise? The older watchers
blink back memories. The crimson lilies
cast their heavy spell. A small bump or two
and docking is complete. This is a go.

Stardate 220701

We are taking our time, doing the rounds quietly
with preparations and farewells. No sadness.
There will be other rendezvous. Almost
it seems as if nothing has changed. It will take time
for the new configurations to bed down.

All the young, strong, handsome crewmen and women
vault into their reconnaissance craft and zoom away
with a waggle of their fins into the future.
Meanwhile we old stagers will retire
to the mother ships, to wait for news.

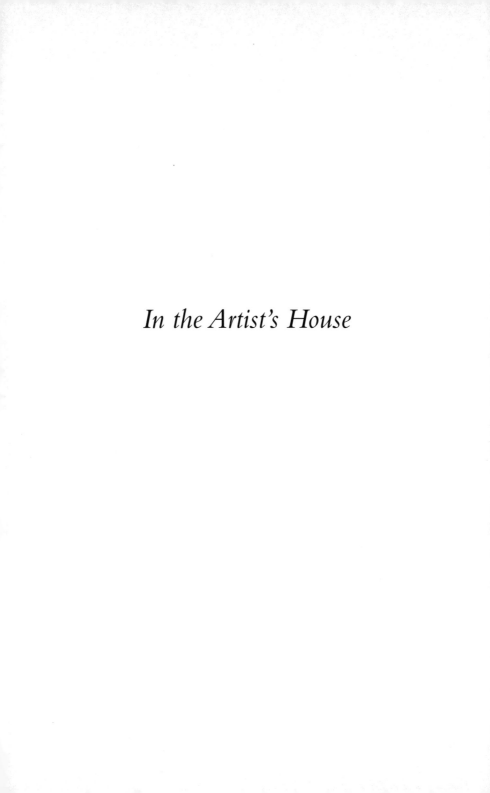

In the Artist's House

Green and Dying

As Dylan prophesied
spring prefigures the fall
that is wept by the dew at dusk.
His own death foretold all
the deaths of things held dear.
Nothing stays as we loved it.

Laughing in his lordship
of the apple towns, did he
already see the great question
that splits humanity:
Do you belong to the land
or must the land belong to you?

Just as the poem said,
Fernhill is forever fled:
the land under occupation
by metal regiments,
the window frames
by plastic gothic.

Between its wings
nestles a conservatory
(mail-order). The wind
guns its engine. Along the stream
chainsaws. Never mind
what happened to the apple trees.

From all vantage points
Fernhill is lost in leaves
like those magic doors
you grow out of
because you can't believe.
Can't believe the hay

Still grows high as the chimney
or that somewhere there's
a Welsh dresser,
lustre jugs, quarry tiles
and an old woman in a pinny
smelling of bibles and scones.

I shall always think of RS

'Ond dôi'r cof amdano ar ei liniau ym mhorth yr eglwys mor bell yn ôl â Manafon. Doedd o ddim i mewn nac allan, ond ar y ffin rhwng y ddau, yn sumbol barod o'r dyn cyfoes . . .'*

Neb R S Thomas

I shall always think of RS
on his knees in the church porch
between altar and bird-flying hills,
halfway from England to the sea.
He worshipped Wales with punishing words,
like a father who says, truthfully,
'This is hurting me more than it hurts you,'
his art in lifelong exile
from his craftsman's *Cymraeg*.
He was one who never flinched
from contradictions, who would neither
step inside and shut the door
against a sea-wind salted with blood,
nor turn his back
on a God who turned his back.

---

* 'But there came a memory of himself on his knees in the church porch, so long ago at Manafon. He was neither inside nor outside, but on the border between the two, a ready symbol of modern man.'

A Bust of Rilke

[For Wendy Earle]

As long as you were here, I did not like
to stare, or question him too closely,
but left him quiet in a corner to settle,
a shy newcomer, while we talked.

I did not ask about his yellow eye
that frightened me a little to begin with
but, as I got to know his gentleness,
embraced, like a friend's hump or stammer.

I saw his ears were bluish, as if
he felt the cold. Like the real Rilke,
his large blue right eye seems forever
outside the window looking in.

For all the marks of pain and sleepless nights
that section his poor face, the gaze
remains stoutly unguarded. A soft sort
of soldier; but poets too have their duty.

Deliver Us from Evil

Such a slight twist
can leave you wrong-
footed off-balance
clutching at nothing

like Epstein's Lucifer
poised at the very edge
of the event horizon, as if
he might still draw back

silk kirtle on the point
of sliding off
bare hips, pleats
barbing his flesh

powerful wings
askew in the updraught
joints and muscles knotted
like the ligature round his breast.

If the light he hoarded
shines on
inside the black hole
there's no way of knowing.

Here, when the daffodils
change in mid-bloom
as if a shadow
had crossed the sun

we can turn instead
to watch the leaves bud.
I wanted an upbeat ending
but some things can't be fixed.

Pietà

Under her marble mantle, the smooth crown
of her head looks swollen, with tears, perhaps,
she is too dignified to shed. The closed lips
pout a little, with angling her face down.

How many currents cross behind that pose,
that almost perfectly controlled expression?
'Is it over already? But you've barely done
lying in my lap, playing with your toes.

Well, this is Motherhood – being ripped open
time and again by your child wrenching away
oblivious, eyes fixed on the horizon.
I have no mother, you used to say.

You never felt how each spear in your side
passed through and wounded me a second later.
Oh, but I could have burst with pride –
all of them looking at my son, the martyr.

Please, let me hold him just a little longer.
What am I meant to do now this is over?'

In the Artist's House

1. Kyffin's Cottage

[For Kyffin Williams]

The cottage stands remote as tales
on a stony spit, licked by the long tongue
of an inlet, lowered on by highlands.
The rows of panes stare darkly
from under limewashed lintels, witnesses
for centuries to shifts of light
and season, framed by the same rim
of lake, toothed edge of sky. Inside
it looks deserted, except for ghosts
and those stone-eyed pictures – slabs
of cliff, wave, cloud, monumental
as Crib Goch. But the painter's here:

A rheumy ex-soldier, heavy-breathing
through Edwardian moustaches,
in an old Burberry to keep his clothes
free of flake white, ochre, lampblack.
He pays rent for his legendary fastness
and always on the nail, is affable
to all comers in his toff's English baritone.
The eternal mountains are slapped on
with a palette knife, one canvas per day.
Of the two, the house looks more the artist,
re-creating deep within itself
the hills which haunt its windows.

2. A Visit to Cantre'r Gwaelod

[For Bim and Arthur Giardelli]

In the old school house, the things she used to know
are slowly unlearning themselves. She passes to and fro
in gallant pursuit of the old easy competence,
achieves tea and cake for guests, responds
as always to the patterns of Arthur's carillon
in an acerbic *sotto voce* counterpoint.

She mourns aloud the long-vanished bells
that once companioned her up in the belfry
where she used to hide and paint
when the strangeness of her life was troublesome.
She knows that younger Bim is also sinking,
along with the words of all the rhymes and tales.

3.Vintrosa Night

[For Monica Sahlin]

Our candelabra-moon, spangled and wreathed,
floated too low in its sky of whitewashed boards
for any but children to polonaise beneath.

Our walls were twilight blue and gilt and lace,
and on the dresser, painted wooden angels
kept watch or flew with enigmatic face.

No need to dream in such a room; our sleep
was bland as a damask counterpane and quiet
as midnight meadows, galaxied with sheep.

A Horsehair Harp

Between thin knees she grips
a length of planking with an oblong hole
strung with three rough plaits, homely
as an old kitchen implement whose use
is now forgotten. The humped bow see-saws
to and fro through resistance, as if
kneading dough or stirring porridge, yet the song
is a keening from under a faraway roof of turf,
a thin wind that mourns across miles of dunes
where the sea breaks black, corniced with surf
under a starless midwinter sky.

Who is returning on horseback through the snow
from the forest of legends? Whose faint lullaby
crosses the strand to him from long ago?

Questioning the Comet

When the Aliens Landed

'Yes, I recall the dark ships disgorging
hundreds of them: sticklike, huge-eyed, staggering
as if gravity were too much for them.

'Their speech was a grunting, thick in the throat,
but they could learn commands and simple tasks.
Doubtless they did not feel the hardship as we would.

'It was striking how later on they would fail
to react when a fist was raised. They seemed
to lack the instinct for self-defence.

'Strange, though: when the whip split
their purple skin, what welled out
was bright red, just like human blood.'

Larsen B

Once this was a continent
defended by a light that grew
harder than rock
as deep as atmospheres.
Cold shielded it against
the puny harlequins
in their toy ships. Cold
that could mummify
in moments, smother
a smudge of life in miles of bandage,
blank out his eyes with cataracts,
lock him like a blood-cell
inside a bleached bone.

It could not last. At first
it was the beaches
where they dyed the snow
engorged the air
with the red stench of flensing.
Now, baby-eyes of meltwater
have opened in the face of ice:
the colour of jailhouse songs
the colour of cyanosis
the colour of a fall
down a crevasse.

Larsen B: an Antarctic ice peninsula.

Loose Ends

1. Getting Away From It All

A body-surfer, the naked woman rises
in one languid ripple, hair waving back
as the bulldozer's edge slides under her.
She flops over and over with the other
sticks of flesh that flail in slow motion
towards the pit, like children and mothers
rolling together down a seaside dune.

We'd have liked to show a bit more respect
but the job was overwhelming, like the stink.
You couldn't help wanting to be quick,
get them all covered up and let them turn
to earth, so the air could be clean again
and we could go back where
even dead mothers are not childless.

2. A Little Bit of Lippy

I was hungry, and you gave me
a gruel that tasted of nothing but goodwill.
I'd been eating worms, but this mush
was too much for me to stomach. Couldn't you
have found me a schmalz herring or a pickle?

I was naked, and you gave me
a blanket. I was still naked,
homeless, a stranger. 'But you're Polish,' you said,
put me with Jew-haters and collaborators
in a German barracks. I ran away, back to Belsen.

And when at last we made treeless Belsen bud
into music, plans, laughter; when we women
stole sanitary towels to make shoulder pads
for our new dresses; when we told jokes against you,
though it was a kind of compliment you felt aggrieved.

But a throne of glory is being prepared
for one among you – the unknown genius
who sent for a boxful of lipsticks.
Now, if we choose, we can die with a scarlet smile
and a gold amulet clutched in our fingers.

Ffynnon Gybi
(St Cybi's Well)

Halfway from the destruction
of the Temple, and across
a continent, this small stone cell
was made, to shelter a spring
ancient beyond calculation.

Halfway between a metalled road
and an Iron-Age hill fort
a cube of lucid riverwater
waits without ripple for anyone
who comes in need of healing.

Niches were cut in the walls
so the weak could sit
awaiting their turn. Shallow steps
lead down into the cistern.
The quiet is a standing pool.

From the wooded hilltop
invisible in mist, sheep groan
quietly. What if all
the migraines of the world
could come as pilgrims?

A curtain of rain
falls across, hiding from view
the distant bay where the river
falls helpless into a seethe
and roar of breakers.

Via Dolorosa

1. The Road to Jerusalem

He said, 'Just over that hill
was the village of Deir Yassin.'

History here speaks four languages.
Two are written on every roadsign:

The square-shouldered one stands above the other
which runs, throwing off diacritics like sweat.

Both are impenetrable to me, but I divine
that everything has two different names.

The third needs an interpreter, who remembers
what once lay over the silent sunbleached hill,

Who can explain the significance
of a tangled row of prickly pears

Who knows by what sleight the mighty Jordan
has been humbled to a runnel of poison-green.

But there is a fourth, written in concrete,
and even I can read these entrails fluently:

The rows of sharks' teeth gaping round the city,
the tarmac incisions that split the bloodless land.

2. Haifa

The crisp-shirted men, the strategists, hold forth
in their seventh-floor boardroom with its heavy table
of glass and blond wood, its commanding views.

'A messy divorce,' they comment drily,
domesticating Armageddon. When we say,
'Tell us your grief,' they only talk louder.

To meet the women, we must abandon pomp
for the clutter of an ordinary classroom. There
waits a plump kibbutznik, mother of six.

In schools, cafés, over garden walls, her neighbours
exchange bigotries. Armageddon lounges at her doorstep
calling her kids with the old lie. But she bars the way.

First one mother, one child, then another and another.
Without names or ranks or rosters or weapons
a No is growing as big as an army.

3. Gaza

Down here in the sunstruck street
you can't see far – a wedge of sparkling sea,
stalls heaped with melons, corn, tomatoes
fat as rich men, traffic, coffee vendors,
shops, jacarandas, pestering barefoot boys
and sand in the gutters. The usual beach scene.

What can the kites see, straining as high
as their strings will let them? From above
the truth seems laid out plain as prison walls.
But hunger can't be seen from the sky. Or anger.
And the kites are stalled in a mockery of free air,
unable to see the gust coming from the future.

They Call it Pink

A mid-afternoon in September. Swollen
oakwoods echo the thunderclouds.
Tunnelling through the trees, an unseen train
hoots in falsetto. But there is no railway line.

Now the whistling and shrieking
come closer, augmented
by hounds and the yelp of a horn.
Still they are invisible. We trudge on.

The path through the woods is churned
by hooves. Off in the gloom a man in green
stands silent and listens. Squalls
hunt overhead, catching and letting us go.

Coming out on the brow, we encounter
two mares, burdened with gentlemen
in rural versions of the bowler hats
they once wore for the bank.

Their whips point across the valley
to a spurt of scarlet like a cut artery,
a quick brown smear of dogs. The howling
has risen to a pitch of triumphal glee.

We walk on, down a lane. Landrovers
roar uphill, cold-eyed. As each one revs past,
anger spurts scarlet in me, like a cut artery.
I hate them for that most of all.

After they've all passed, we half-glimpse
further down the hill the silhouette
of a deer, slipping without haste
across the lane into sanctuary.

Road Sign

The tread-print in the verge
spells out in naked mud
the way the future slid
out of control and into
a limbo of silent struggle
as if you thought the moment
a wheel within your grip.

But the moment won't respond,
slips sideways, snatches your air,
leaves you to gasp in its ebb
till you find out what you are –
a cuttlefish, beached and drying?
or will the wave break over
and time resume its flow?

At last the breaker crashes –
you murmur at its violence;
you're used to politer handling.
You're spun, a helpless plankton,
and dumped into a ditch.
The car's onrush is snuffed.
You are still alive.

What's meant to happen next?
If you were dead or injured
you wouldn't have to think.
You switch off the ignition,
release your belt with care,
step from the tilted wreck
back into your element.

A robin whistles, indifferent.
You haven't a bruise to show
yet nothing tastes the same –
no landmarks, and you'll have
to relearn how to swim.

A balding Nausicaa
in navy suit and crombie
pulls up and offers help.
He gently drives you home.
Your husband doesn't cavil
that you've written off the motor.
You're grateful for these things.

Soon time will start running again,
green will close over the wake
you left beside the tarmac.
But birdsong now will pierce you
and this will be a sign.

Spring Equinox

1. Traethgwyn

The wind has fallen so light
the sea looks clingfilmed, against gullshit
perhaps, or the air's infections.

Sky's only faintly hazed; its blue
seems unending, though the ancients knew
it was mere glaze inside a hollow night.

Chiffchaff, dunnock, robin, wren
tootle over and over their tuneless tunes
oblivious as Brueghel ploughmen.

Yet again, the odd bee and the flush of green
as if all events were harmless and came round each year.
As if earth cliffs could stay just as they are.

2. Cei Bach

The bay is a cup of sunned milk below woods,
below rock ziggurats; in each patterned ledge
gorse, spindlebush or gulls are wedged.

Two boys with rods are hectored at the water's edge
by Grandpa, till a dogfish contorting in mid-air
reels in Gran with Polaroid from her canvas chair.

A dry creek of boulders dwindles into nowhere.
I place a trove of pebbles near the ebb-line
where the tide will wash them rose, onyx, serpentine.

The fish is freed; we take this for a sign.
You join my game, toeing a boy-scout arrow.
There'll be fresh jewels next time the tide is low.

Questioning the Comet

Having calculated
your five-thousand-year
orbit and the exact
date of your arrival, scientists
gave you a name, absurd
and human, like a duo
of stand-up comics or
a cartoon knock-out
as if we had you pat.
But you plunge past
self-sufficient
down your own light-tunnel
into an infinite night,
just another circuit
in a series beyond number
where we can never follow
caught as we are
in an eye-blink of time
gasp of air gulp of water.
Does it matter how
each of us behaves
between the opening
and closing of the lid?
I seize the rare chance
to question a comet
in puffs of night breath, like
a dandelion clock
ticktocking between
challenge and absolution –
It matters. It matters not.
It matters. It matters not.
It matters . . .